CONTENTS

GO MARINERS!

The Seattle Mariners compete in Major League Baseball's (MLB) **American League** (AL). They play in the AL West **division**, along with the Houston Astros, Los Angeles Angels, Oakland Athletics, and Texas Rangers. Seattle fans are some of the loudest and most passionate in all of baseball. The Mariners are the only MLB team that has never played in the **World Series**. Their fans hope this will change very soon! Let's learn more about the Seattle Mariners!

AMERICAN LEAGUE WEST DIVISION

Houston Astros	Los Angeles Angels	Oakland Athletics	Seattle Mariners	Texas Rangers

The Mariners celebrate a 3–1 win over the Texas Rangers in 2022. ▶

SEATTLE MARINERS

JOSH ANDERSON

childsworld.com

Published by The Child's World®
800-599-READ • childsworld.com

Photography Credits
Cover: ©Bob Levey/Stringer/Getty Images; page 5: ©Steph Chambers/Staff/Getty Images; page 6: ©Doug Griffin/Contributor/Getty Images; page 9: ©Lane Turner/The Boston Globe/Contributor/Getty Images; page 10: ©Steph Chambers/Staff/Getty Images; page 12: ©Steph Chambers/Staff/Getty Images; page 12: ©Denis Poroy/Contributor/Getty Images; page 13: ©Steph Chambers/Staff/Getty Images; page 13: ©Focus on Sport/Contributor/Getty Images; page 14: ©Steph Chambers/Staff/Getty Images; page 15: ©Stephen Brashear/Stringer/Getty Images; page 16: ©Ron Vesely/Contributor/Getty Images; page 16: ©Jacob de Golish /Stringer/Getty Images; page 17: ©Ron Vesely/Contributor/Getty Images; page 17: ©Mitchell Layton/Contributor/Getty Images; page 18: ©B Bennett/Contributor/Getty Images; page 18: ©Stephen Dunn/Staff/Getty Images; page 19: ©Otto Greule Jr./Contributor/ALLSPORT/Getty Images: page 19: ©Daniel Shirey/Stringer/Getty Images; page 20: ©Carmen Mandato/Staff/Getty Images; page 20: ©Steph Chambers/Staff/Getty Images; page 21: ©Steph Chambers/Staff/Getty Images; page 21: ©Steph Chambers/Staff/Getty Images; page 22: ©Otto Greule Jr./Stringer/Getty Images; page 23: ©The Sporting News/Contributor/Getty Images; page 25: ©Dan Levine/Stringer/AFP/Getty Images; page 26: ©Jason O. Watson/Contributor/Getty Images; page 29: ©Lonnie Major/Contributor/Allsport/Getty Images

ISBN Information
9781503888500 (Reinforced Library Binding)
9781503890770 (Portable Document Format)
9781503892019 (Online Multi-user eBook)
9781503893252 (Electronic Publication)

LCCN
2023950247

Printed in the United States of America

ABOUT THE AUTHOR

Josh Anderson has published over 50 books for children and young adults. His two boys are the greatest joys in his life. His hobbies include coaching his sons in youth basketball, no-holds-barred games of Apples to Apples, and taking long family walks. His favorite MLB team is a secret he'll never share!

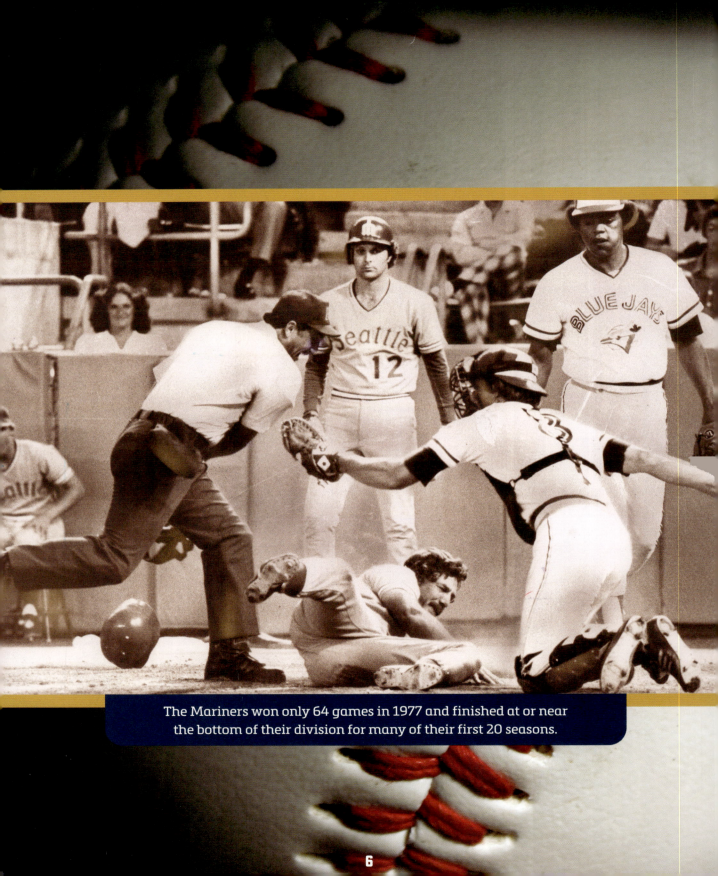

The Mariners won only 64 games in 1977 and finished at or near the bottom of their division for many of their first 20 seasons.

BECOMING THE MARINERS

The Mariners began play in 1977 as a new team in the AL. For the first 10 years of the team's history, Seattle finished near the bottom of the AL West division. In 1989, the team picked Ken Griffey Jr. in the MLB **Draft**. He helped change the team's fortunes. The team's first winning record came in 1991. Seattle made it to the **playoffs** for the first time in 1995. Then, in 2001, the Mariners tied the MLB record for wins in a season when they finished with a 116–46 record. In recent years, outfielder Julio Rodríguez has become a superstar and helped bring the Mariners back to the playoffs again.

BY THE NUMBERS

T he Mariners have accomplished a lot on the baseball field. Below is some information on some of the greatest Mariners teams of all time.

SEATTLE MARINERS STATISTICS

MOST WINS IN A SEASON

YEAR	WINS	LOSSES	WIN %
2001	116	46	.716
2002	93	69	.574
2003	93	69	.574
2000	91	71	.562.
2022	90	72	.556
2021	90	72	.556
1997	90	72	.556

AL WEST DIVISION TITLES

YEAR		
1995	1997	2001

Mariners outfielders Ken Griffey Jr. and his father, Ken Griffey Sr., made MLB history in 1990 as the first ▶ father and son to appear in the same lineup.

T-Mobile Park has a retractable roof, which means the team can close the roof over the field on game days when the weather is rainy or cold.

GAME DAY

The Mariners have had two home stadiums. From 1977 until 1999, the team played in the Kingdome. They shared the building with the National Football League's Seattle Seahawks and the National Basketball Association's Seattle SuperSonics. In 1999, the team moved into T-Mobile Park, which was called Safeco Field for many years. On game days, the ballpark holds nearly 48,000 fans. On their way inside, fans can see a large statue of baseball legend Ken Griffey Jr.

WE'RE FAMOUS

In *Little Big League,* a 12-year-old boy named Billy Heywood becomes the owner of the Minnesota Twins. During a key moment of the movie, Heywood's Twins battle the Mariners in a tied game. Tied, that is, until Ken Griffey Jr. (playing himself in the movie) steps up to the plate. Griffey hits a monster home run to give Seattle the lead.

UNIFORM

HOME

AWAY

ALTERNATE UNIFORM

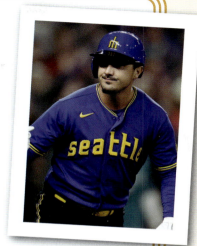

An alternate uniform has colors, lettering, and other details that are different from a team's regular season home and away uniforms. The Mariners' City Connect uniform honors the team's past. The hat includes the **trident** "M" logo that the team used during the early 1980s. The jersey reads "Seattle" and is similar to the jersey worn by the Seattle Pilots, a team that played one season before moving to Milwaukee and being renamed the Milwaukee Brewers.

TRULY WEIRD

A baseball diamond has two foul lines extending out from home plate. In the infield, any ball that stops in between the lines is considered a fair ball and is in play. Any ball outside the lines is foul. In a game in 1981, Kansas City Royals batter Amos Otis hit a slow-rolling ball that stopped right on the third base foul line. Otis reached first base before any Mariner could pick the ball up. Hoping to turn the ball into a foul ball, Mariners third baseman Lenny Randle got down on the ground and used his mouth to blow the ball into foul territory. While his idea was certainly creative, the umpires weren't convinced and called it a fair ball.

The Mariner Moose became Seattle's mascot after the team invited local children to send in mascot ideas in 1990. The team chose the Moose from more than 2,500 suggestions from kids ages 14 and under.

TEAM SPIRIT

Going to a Mariners game at T-Mobile Park can be loads of fun. Fans cheer during the game, hoping the team can light up the downtown Seattle sky with the blue "W" on the outside of the ballpark. This happens each time the Mariners win. Fans also love when a player hits a home run. When a player hits a homer, his teammates give him a trident to hold during the dugout celebration. And at every home game, the team's mascot, the Mariner Moose, entertains the crowd. The Moose first appeared in 1990 and has been having a blast at home games ever since.

Julio Rodríguez carries the trident into the dugout after a home run against the Houston Astros in 2023. ▶

HEROES OF HISTORY

KEN GRIFFEY JR.
CENTER FIELDER
1989–1999; 2009–2010

Ken Griffey Jr. may have been the most popular athlete in Seattle sports history. Griffey made his first appearance as a Mariner at age 19 and delighted fans in the city for 13 of his 22 MLB seasons. In 1997, he was named AL MVP. Griffey led the AL in home runs four times. He won 10 **Gold Glove** Awards and was named an **All-Star** 13 times in his career. Griffey retired with 630 career home runs, which ranks seventh all-time. He is a member of the Baseball **Hall of Fame**.

FÉLIX HERNÁNDEZ
PITCHER
2005–2019

For much of his 15-year career, Mariners fans would celebrate the days when "King Félix" Hernández was scheduled to pitch. Hernández was one of baseball's top pitchers, twice leading the league in **earned run average** (ERA). From 2009 through 2014, Hernández had six straight seasons with more than 200 strikeouts. In 2010, he won the Cy Young Award, which is presented to the AL's top pitcher. He was chosen as an All-Star six times.

RANDY JOHNSON
PITCHER
1989–1998

Nicknamed "The Big Unit" for his incredible 6 foot, 10 inch (208.3 centimeter) height, Randy Johnson was likely the most intimidating pitcher of his generation. As a Mariner, Johnson won the 1995 Cy Young Award, the first of five he earned in his career. He led the league in strikeouts nine times, four while playing for Seattle. Johnson had 4,875 strikeouts in his career, which is the second-most of any player in baseball history. He also retired with 303 wins, which ranks 22nd all-time. A 10-time All-Star, Johnson was chosen for the Baseball Hall of Fame in 2015.

EDGAR MARTINEZ
DESIGNATED HITTER
1987–2004

Edgar Martinez spent his entire 18-year career in Seattle. During that time, he led the league in **batting average** twice, **doubles** twice, and **runs batted in** (RBIs) once. In 2001, Martinez batted .306 and hit 23 home runs as a key part of the Mariners' team that tied the all-time record for wins in a season. Martinez was chosen as an All-Star seven times in his career. After he retired, he was honored with entry into the Baseball Hall of Fame.

BIG DAYS

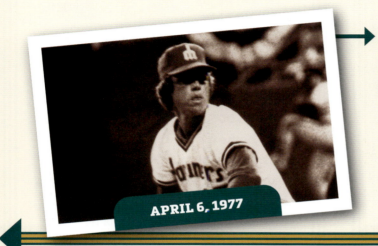

APRIL 6, 1977

In the team's first game ever, the Mariners lose to the California Angels 7–0.

The Mariners defeat the New York Yankees 6–5 in Game 5 of the AL Division Series (ALDS) in extra innings. They advance to the American **League Championship Series** (ALCS).

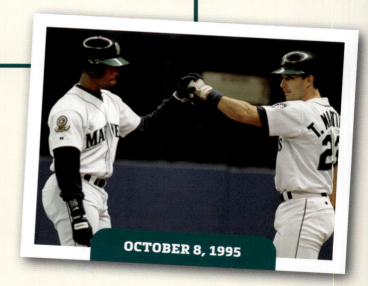

OCTOBER 8, 1995

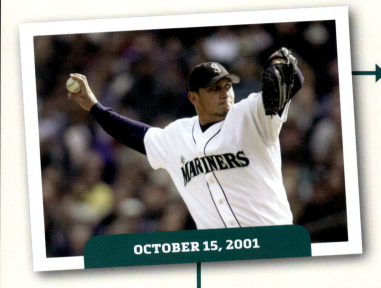

OCTOBER 15, 2001

Seattle defeats the Cleveland Guardians 3–1 in Game 5 of the ALDS to advance to the ALCS for only the third time in team history.

The Mariners return to the playoffs for the first time in more than 20 years. Although they lose to the Houston Astros 8–7, it's a moment of celebration for Seattle fans.

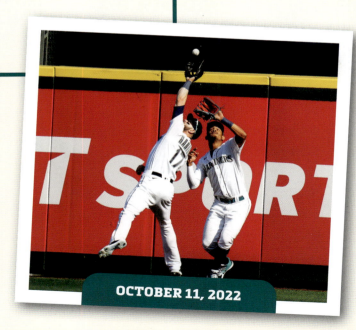

OCTOBER 11, 2022

MODERN-DAY MARVELS

LUIS CASTILLO
PITCHER
2022–PRESENT

After six seasons with the Cincinnati Reds, Luis Castillo was traded to the Mariners during the 2022 season. In addition to his skill on the pitching mound, Castillo is known for rarely missing a game. He has led the league in games started twice, including in 2023, his first full season with the Mariners. In 2022, Castillo helped the Mariners reach the playoffs for the first time in more than 20 years. He has been chosen as an All-Star three times in his career.

J. P. CRAWFORD
SHORTSTOP
2019–PRESENT

J. P. Crawford joined the Mariners in 2019. Since 2020, he's started most of the team's games at shortstop. That year, he won a Gold Glove Award for his amazing defense. Crawford has improved as a hitter throughout his career. In 2021, he finished eighth in the AL with 169 hits. In 2023, he hit 19 home runs and led the AL with 94 walks.

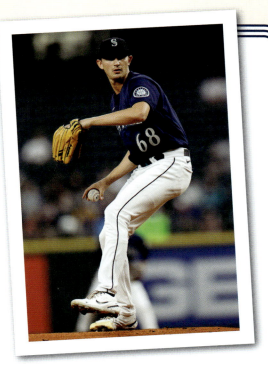

GEORGE KIRBY
PITCHER
2022–PRESENT

The Mariners picked George Kirby in the first round of the 2019 MLB Draft. Since joining the team in 2022, Kirby has become one of the top young pitchers in baseball. In 2023, he finished sixth in the AL with 13 wins and sixth in ERA with 3.35. Kirby also gave up the fewest walks per nine innings of any pitcher in the AL. That year, he was chosen as an All-Star for the first time.

JULIO RODRÍGUEZ
CENTER FIELDER
2022–PRESENT

Julio Rodríguez is one of the most exciting and dynamic young players in all of baseball. He took the MLB by storm as a **rookie** in 2022 when he batted .285 with 28 home runs and 25 stolen bases. Rodríguez was named the AL Rookie of the Year that season and played in the All-Star Game. He improved on his home run and steals totals in 2023 and was named an All-Star again.

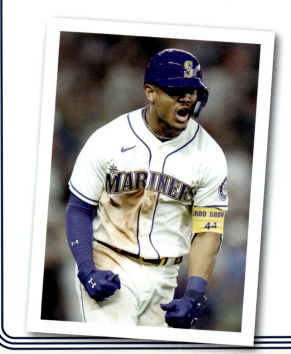

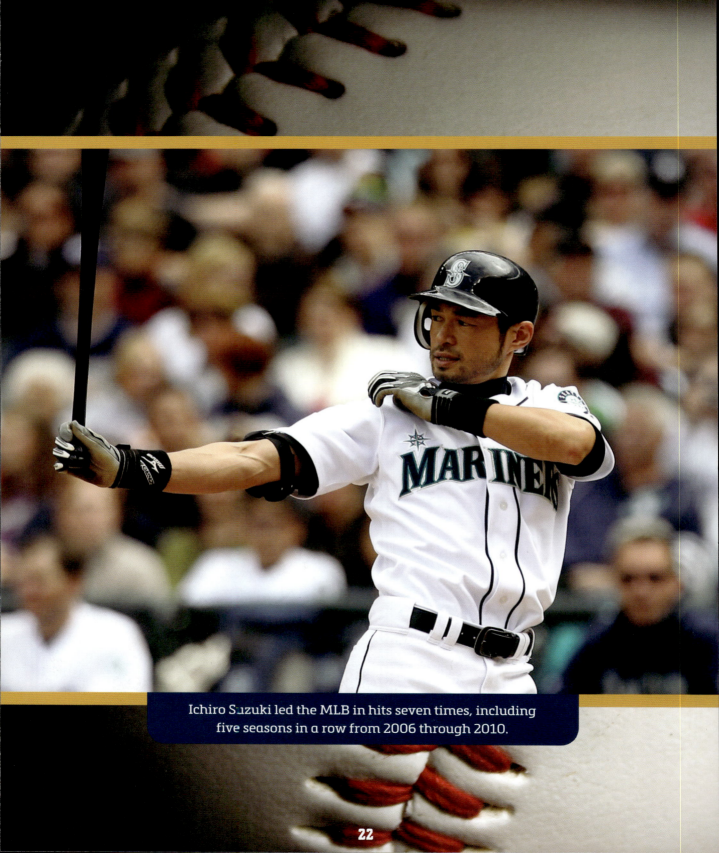

Ichiro Suzuki led the MLB in hits seven times, including five seasons in a row from 2006 through 2010.

GREATEST OF ALL TIME

Ichiro Suzuki joined the Mariners in 2001 after playing nine seasons in Japan's Nippon Professional Baseball league. In 2004, Ichiro, who goes by his first name on the field, set the single-season record for hits in a season with 262. No other player in history has led their league in hits five straight seasons. His 10 straight seasons with 200 hits is also an MLB record. Ichiro won the Rookie of the Year and AL MVP Awards in 2001. He also won 10 Gold Glove Awards and was chosen as an All-Star 10 times during his career.

FAN FAVORITE

Although he was only named an All-Star once in his career, powerful hitter Jay Buhner amazed Mariners fans for the 14 seasons he played in the city of Seattle. Fans especially loved Buhner's hitting skills. He was a top hitter on the 1995 team, which made the first playoff appearance in Mariners history. In that season's AL Division Series, Buhner had 11 hits in five games to help the Mariners defeat the New York Yankees.

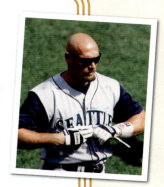

THE BIG GAME

OCTOBER 6, 2001
NEXT-TO-LAST GAME OF THE
REGULAR SEASON

In order to tie the record for the most wins ever in a season, Seattle needed to win one of its final two games of 2001. In the bottom of the first inning, Mariners second baseman Bret Boone hit a home run to deep right field. The game remained close all the way into the final innings, with the Mariners clinging to a 1–0 lead. In the bottom of the ninth with two outs, Alex Rodriguez, former Mariner and one of the game's most feared hitters, stepped to the plate. Mariners closer Kazuhiro Sasaki struck out Rodriguez, and the Mariners tied baseball's all-time record of 116 wins in a season.

Seattle players celebrate their 116th win of the 2001 season, the most in team history. ▶

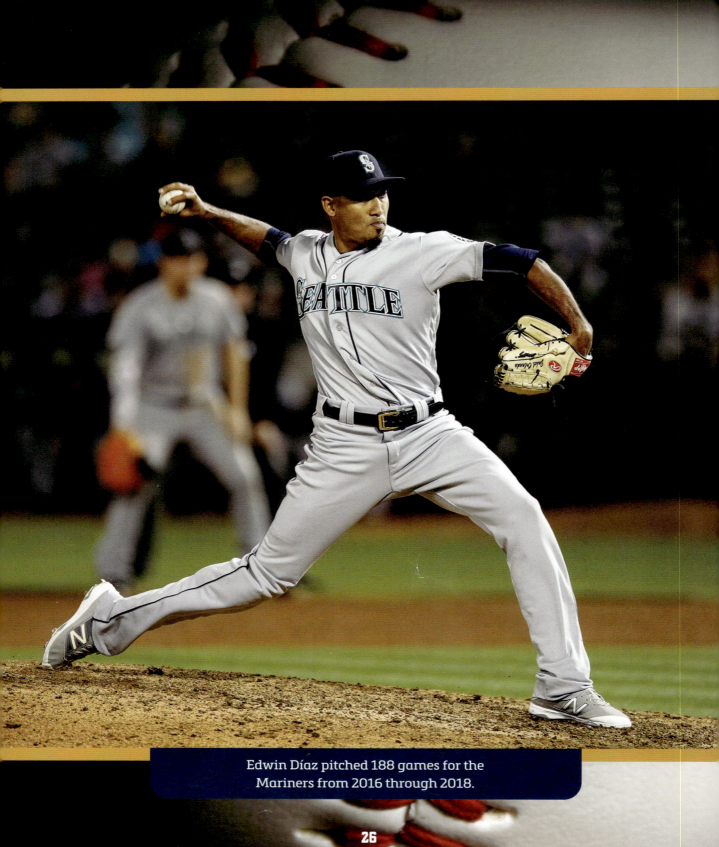

Edwin Díaz pitched 188 games for the
Mariners from 2016 through 2018.

AMAZING FEATS

SINGLE-SEASON BATTING RECORDS

STATISTIC	PLAYER	NUMBER	YEAR
Batting average	Ichiro Suzuki	.372	2004
Home runs	Ken Griffey Jr.	56	1997
	Ken Griffey Jr.	56	1998
RBI	Ken Griffey Jr.	147	1997
Runs	Alex Rodriguez	141	1996
Hits	Ichiro Suzuki	262	2004
Singles	Ichiro Suzuki	225	2004
Doubles	Alex Rodriguez	54	1996
Triples	Ichiro Suzuki	12	2005
Extra base hits	Ken Griffey Jr.	93	1997
Stolen bases	Harold Reynolds	60	1987
Hitting streak	Ichiro Suzuki	27 games	2009
Walks	Edgar Martinez	123	1996
Strikeouts	Eugenio Suarez	214	2023
Team HR	Team	264	1997

Through 3/19/24

SINGLE-SEASON PITCHING RECORDS

STATISTIC	PLAYER	NUMBER	YEAR
Wins	Jamie Moyer	21	2003
Strikeouts	Randy Johnson	308	1993
ERA	Félix Hernández	2.14	2014
Saves	Edwin Díaz	57	2018

ALL-TIME BEST

MOST HOME RUNS

1	Ken Griffey Jr.	417
2	Edgar Martinez	309
3	Jay Buhner	307
4	Kyle Seager	242
5	Alex Rodriguez	189

HIGHEST BATTING AVERAGE

1	Ichiro Suzuki	.321
2	Edgar Martinez	.312
3	Alex Rodriguez	.309
4	Phil Bradley	.301
5	Robinson Canó	.296
	Tom Paciorek	.296

MOST STOLEN BASES

1	Ichiro Suzuki	438
2	Julio Cruz	290
3	Harold Reynolds	228
4	Ken Griffey Jr.	167
5	Alex Rodriguez	133

MOST RBI

1	Edgar Martinez	1,261
2	Ken Griffey Jr.	1,216
3	Jay Buhner	951
4	Kyle Seager	807
5	Alvin Davis	667

MOST PITCHING WINS

1	Félix Hernández	169
2	Jamie Moyer	145
3	Randy Johnson	130
4	Freddy Garcia	76
5	Mark Langston	74

MOST SAVES

1	Kazuhiro Sasaki	129
2	Edwin Díaz	109
3	J. J. Putz	101
4	Mike Schooler	98
5	David Aardsma	69

In his first season with the Mariners, Alvin Davis was an All-Star and the AL Rookie of the Year in 1984.

GLOSSARY

All-Star (ALL STAR) An All-Star is a player chosen as one of the best in their sport.

American League (uh-MAYR-ih-kun LEEG) The American League is one of the two groups of teams in Major League Baseball. The other is the National League. The winner of each league competes in the World Series every season.

batting average (BAT-ting AV-rij) Batting average is a three-digit number representing the percentage of times at bat that a hitter has reached base without getting out.

division (dih-VIZSH-un) A division is a group of five teams that compete with each other to have the best record each season and advance to the playoffs.

double (DUH-bul) A double is a hit that results in the batter reaching second base.

draft (DRAFT) A draft is a period of time when teams take turns choosing new players.

earned run average (ERND RUN AV-rij) ERA is a three-digit number representing how many runs a pitcher would give up on average in a nine-inning game.

Gold Glove (GOLD GLUV) The Gold Glove is an award given each season to the best fielder at each position in each league.

Hall of Fame (HAHL of FAYM) The Baseball Hall of Fame is a museum located in Cooperstown, New York. The best players in the game are honored with plaques in the building listing their accomplishments on the field.

League Championship Series (LEEG CHAM-pee-un-ship SEER-eez) The League Championship Series is a playoff series between two teams from either the National or American League to decide which team will win the pennant and go to the World Series.

playoffs (PLAY-offs) Playoffs are games that take place after the end of the regular season to determine each year's championship team.

rookie (ROOK-ee) A rookie is a player in his first year.

run batted in (RUN BAT-ted IN) An RBI is a hit that causes a teammate to score a run.

trident (TRY-dent) A trident is a spear with three points that is usually associated with the Greek water god Poseidon.

World Series (WORLD SEER-eez) The World Series is a set of games played at the end of the season between the winners of the American League and National League.

FAST FACTS

◆ Lou Pinella, who managed the Mariners from 1993 to 2002, holds the team record with 840 wins as a manager.

◆ Félix Hernández was Seattle's starting pitcher on Opening Day 11 times. That's more than any other pitcher in team history.

◆ The Mariners have honored two of their players by retiring their numbers. That means no Mariner will ever wear that number on their jersey. They are Edgar Martinez (11) and Ken Griffey Jr. (24).

◆ Randy Johnson pitched the first no-hitter in Mariners history on June 2, 1990, against the Detroit Tigers.

ONE STRIDE FURTHER

◆ Pete Rose is baseball's all-time hits leader with 4,256 in his Major League career. The Mariners' Ichiro Suzuki had 3,089 hits in the Major Leagues. But he also had 1,278 hits in Japan for a total of 4,367 as a professional. Which of the two players do you think has the right to claim the title of baseball's all-time "Hit King"? Write down your reasons.

◆ In baseball, a hitter who bats .300 or higher for an entire season is considered very successful. A .300 average is equal to getting a hit only three out of 10 times at bat. Think about whether there are other examples in sports where you can be "successful" even if you're unsuccessful most of the time.

◆ Based on what you learned in this book, what do you think it takes for a team to win the World Series? Is hitting the most important thing, or is it pitching? Maybe it's fielding? What about teamwork? Discuss your opinion with a friend.

◆ Ask friends and family members to name their favorite sport to watch and their favorite sport to play. Keep track and make a graph to see which sports are the most popular.

FIND OUT MORE

IN THE LIBRARY

Buckley Jr., James. *It's a Numbers Game! Baseball: The Math Behind the Perfect Pitch, the Game-Winning Grand Slam, and So Much More!* Washington, DC: National Geographic Kids, 2021.

Martin, Andrew. *Baseball's Greatest Players: 10 Baseball Biographies for New Readers.* Emeryville, CA: Rockridge Press, 2022.

Whiting, Jim. *The Story of the Seattle Mariners.* Mankato, MN: The Creative Company, 2021.

ON THE WEB

Visit our website for links about the Seattle Mariners:
childsworld.com/links

Note to Parents, Teachers, Caregivers, and Librarians: We routinely verify our web links to make sure they are safe and active sites. So encourage your readers to check them out!

INDEX